Locked Out: The Paywall Killing American Soccer

C. Trent Boop

Published by C. Trent Boop, 2025.

Table of Contents

Locked Out: The Paywall Killing American Soccer

C. TRENT BOOP

Christopher Trent Boop

Copyright

Foreword

Soccer, the world's game, holds within it the power to unite, uplift, and transform lives. From the bustling streets of Rio to the concrete courts of Paris, the game has long been a ladder for the working class—a path to greatness that begins not with privilege, but with passion. But in the United States, that path is increasingly blocked by something as unrelenting as any defender: a paywall.

In *Locked Out: The Paywall Killing American Soccer*, the stark truth is laid bare—America's soccer system isn't broken by accident. It was built this way.

This book shines a much-needed spotlight on the systemic failure of U.S. club soccer to prioritize talent over access. Across the country, thousands of promising young players are being priced out before they ever get a fair chance to compete. Pay-to-play clubs dominate the youth landscape, charging families thousands of dollars a year for what should be a right, not a privilege—the chance to play, to grow, to dream.

Meanwhile, recreational leagues, the first touchpoint for many kids, are vanishing. Once-vibrant programs in parks and neighborhoods are drying up, victims of budget cuts and disinterest. In their place, elite clubs flourish, offering pathways only to those who can afford the toll.

Contrast that with AAU basketball, where low-income participation isn't a problem to be solved—it's a priority. Coaches and programs actively recruit in underserved communities. They scout playgrounds, not portfolios. They recognize that greatness doesn't come from affluence, it comes from hunger, grit, and opportunity. Soccer in America could do the same. But too often, it chooses not to.

Internationally, nations like France, Brazil, and Germany have figured it out. Their systems are built to discover and develop talent wherever it lives, especially in places where hope is scarce and the drive to succeed burns brightest. They subsidize development. They invest in infrastructure. They make sure that if a kid can play, the door is open.

This book is a call to action—for parents, coaches, clubs, and the highest levels of U.S. Soccer and Major League Soccer. It is time to change the paradigm. Time to rebuild our soccer system not around wealth but around will. Not around exclusivity, but equity.

If we truly want to compete on the world stage—not just with dollars, but with heart—we need to tear down the paywall that is locking out the next generation of American soccer talent. The future is out there, playing barefoot in apartment courtyards and kicking balls made of rolled-up socks. It's time we went looking for them.

— C. Trent Boop

Acknowledgement

This book was born out of frustration, but also out of hope. Hope that by naming the barriers, challenging the system, and telling the truth, we can help shape a better future for American soccer.

To the rec league organizers, the community volunteers, and the coaches who refuse to give up on underserved neighborhoods - you are the heartbeat of what soccer in the U.S. should be. Thank you for continuing to fight for access, equity, and joy in the game.

To those working behind the scenes - journalists, academics, and advocates - who've tracked the rise of pay-to-play, the decline of rec soccer, and the missed opportunities of U.S. youth development, your work laid the foundation for this one.

Finally, this book is dedicated to the kids who never got the chance - not because they couldn't play, but because no one ever came looking for them. May this work spark a change that ensures their stories aren't repeated.

The future of American soccer doesn't belong to the wealthy, it belongs to the willing. Let's open the gates.

- C. Trent Boop

Dedication

To my dad, Terry Boop.

Twelve years ago, I was blessed to take my first youth sports head coaching job, leading a rowdy group of first and second-grade soccer players. I decided to ask my dad, Terry Boop, if he'd want to be my assistant...those who know him understand that he is a busy man, so I initially hesitated because I didn't want to take him away from anything else. That decision was the best I've made as a coach.

My dad has been by my side during the ups and downs of an awesome journey...through soccer, basketball, t-ball, and softball. He was there to pick up my sunglasses when I threw them on the ground because I was mad at the refs. He made sure I maintained perspective when I got angry at opposing coaches. He was there to help kids when they needed a pep talk and after they twisted an ankle. He was a ride for players who didn't have one. He embodied what being a good man looks like to all the athletes on our teams.

This book is dedicated to you - not only for the years of unwavering support, but for being the kind of coach, father, and mentor I aspire to be. Thank you for walking my journey with me.

I love you, Dad.

Chapter 1: The One Season That Changed Everything

Jeremy Parker had never been good at anything—at least, that's what he told himself. He wasn't the smartest kid in his sixth-grade class, nor the funniest, and he certainly wasn't the strongest. Most days, he kept his head down, avoiding the kids who had figured out early on that shy boy made easy targets.

Then, that summer, his mom signed him up for soccer.

Linda Parker had always believed that sports were good for kids—not for winning, scholarships, or raising the next star athlete, but for movement, teamwork, and, in Jeremy's case, perhaps—just perhaps—finding a place where he belonged. She'd noticed how he shrank at school, how he hesitated at lunch tables, how his eyes stayed fixed on the ground. So, when she spotted the flyer for the Lincoln Park Youth Soccer League at the grocery store, its bolded "No experience necessary!" catching her eye, she took a chance.

At $75 for the season, it was manageable even on her tight budget. The league provided uniforms and balls, and games were held at the nearby park. She didn't know if he'd like it, but it was worth a try.

A New Beginning

Jeremy didn't want to go to the first practice. He mumbled something about feeling sick, but Linda gently nudged him into the car.

When they arrived at the park, kids were already sprinting across the grass, sending soccer balls flying in every direction, their laughter buzzing in the warm evening air. Parents stood in small groups, chatting as they watched. The coach—a man in his forties with a kind smile and a weathered whistle around his neck—clapped his hands.

"Alright, team! Let's bring it in!"

Jeremy hovered at the edge of the field, frozen in place. The coach spotted him and strode over.

"You must be Jeremy," he said, extending a hand. "I'm Coach Dave. Glad you're here."

Jeremy shook his head, eyes darting away.

The first practice was a disaster. Jeremy had never played soccer before, and it showed. He tripped over the ball, ran the wrong way, and whiffed every kick. But the strangest thing? Nobody laughed. Instead, Carlos—one of the team's best players—jogged over after a terrible miss and clapped him on the shoulder.

"You'll get it," he said, grinning. "Just keep trying."

For the first time in forever, Jeremy felt like he belonged.

By the third practice, he had started to show improvement. By the first game, he wasn't great—but he wasn't terrible, either. Playing defense, he chased down opponents, blocked shots, and ran harder than he'd ever thought possible. When his team won, a fierce, unfamiliar pride surged through him.

Soon, Saturday mornings became the highlight of his week. He loved the crisp scent of morning grass, the easy jokes during warm-ups, the way his mom's voice rang out from the sidelines. For the first time, he had real friends. Carlos invited him over after games, and before long, they were inseparable.

Jeremy had finally found his place.

And then, just like that, it was gone.

The End of the Line

One evening in early spring, Linda came home from work with bad news. "The league isn't running this year," she said, setting her purse down. There weren't enough children signed up.

Jeremy frowned. "What do you mean? What happened to everyone?"

Linda hesitated, debating how much to say. She had overheard other parents talking. A new club team had started in town, promising "elite" coaching and exposure to higher levels of play. Many families had pulled their kids from the rec league to join it, despite the hefty price tag of $2,500 per season.

Jeremy didn't know any of that. He just knew that soccer, the one thing that had made him feel like he was worth something, was gone.

He called Carlos that night. "Are you playing somewhere else?" he asked, his voice tight.

"Yeah," Carlos said. "I made the Strikers."

Jeremy swallowed. "Oh, that's cool."

"You should try out!" Carlos said. "It's fun."

Jeremy wanted to. Desperately. But he already knew the answer.

"Yeah... I don't think I can," he said.

That summer, the soccer fields sat empty. No kids were running, no laughter, no parents cheering—just grass and silence.

And Jeremy? He went back to walking with his head down.

Reflections & Data Integration

Jeremy's story isn't unique. Across America, recreational sports programs are vanishing as pay-to-play clubs take over. According to the Aspen Institute, participation in youth sports has plummeted among lower-income families—children from households earning under $25,000 are half as likely to play organized sports as their wealthier peers.

The culprit? The rise of elite club teams charging thousands per season, shutting out families who can't afford the steep fees. Over the past twenty years, nonprofit community leagues like Jeremy's have withered while for-profit organizations peddle promises of elite training and college recruitment—often at prices that exclude most kids.

The cruel irony? Despite skyrocketing spending on youth soccer, the United States still lags internationally. Nations like Brazil, France, and Germany cultivate talent through academies that scout players based on their skills, not their bank accounts. Meanwhile, America's paywall system too often reserves opportunities for those who can buy them.

Interview: A Mother's Perspective

To understand the real-world impact, I spoke with Amanda Lewis, a single mother forced to make an impossible choice for her soccer-loving son, Tyler.

"When our local league folded, the only option left was a travel team—over $3,000 a year," she said. "We couldn't swing it. So he quit."

I asked how Tyler took it. Amanda's voice tightened. "He lost a piece of himself. Started hiding in his room, glued to video games. Never clicked with another sport." A pause. "It broke my heart."

Her story isn't unique. When sports become a luxury, the kids who need them most—the ones who find a sense of belonging on those fields—are the first to be pushed out.

Looking Ahead

Jeremy's story is only part of the problem. Next, we'll expose how poor coaching and blatant favoritism push kids out of sports - even when money isn't an issue. Meet Liam, a talented player whose own father's coaching sabotages his love of the game. And we'll reveal the uncomfortable truths about why so many promising young athletes walk away before ever realizing their full potential.

Chapter 2: The Coach's Son

Liam Porter didn't choose soccer—it chose him. Or rather, his father did.

From the moment Liam took his first steps, a soccer ball was waiting for him. Greg Porter, a former Division III player who treated the sport like scripture, saw his son as both legacy and proving ground. By the time Liam turned five, Greg had assembled a ragtag neighborhood team—a dad-coached experiment fueled more by fervor than finesse.

But when Liam hit ten, Greg's ambitions outgrew the rec league. He rebranded a travel team as the Summit FC Predators, installing himself as architect of a vision only he could see.

For Liam, it became the ultimate double-edged sword: a front-row seat to the game he loved, with his father's shadow stretching across every blade of grass.

The Weight of Expectations

By twelve, everyone on the team knew the unspoken rule: Coach Greg's son was untouchable.

Liam played every minute of every game—even when his legs shook with exhaustion. He took every penalty kick—even when others had better shots. Mistakes? If Liam made one, it was "no big deal." If another kid did, they faced Greg's blistering criticism.

It didn't matter who was faster or more creative. Liam was the centerpiece. The playmaker. The non-negotiable star.

And Liam despised it.

The truth gnawed at him: he was decent, not exceptional. His teammates knew it. He knew it. But the worst part came after games, when his dad would dissect his every misstep over dinner, leaving Liam wondering if he even liked soccer anymore.

All he wanted was for his father to see him, not just another piece on his coaching chessboard.

Losing the Team

The whispers started first.

"Why does Liam never come off?" Jack, a defender, muttered after another brutal loss.

Ryan didn't bother lowering his voice. "Because Coach is his dad."

Snickers rippled through the carpool van. Everyone knew—they'd just stopped pretending otherwise.

By the end of the season, three players had walked away. The most significant loss was Derek Wilson, their star striker.

Derek's parents had bitten their tongues for months. Their son led the team in goals yet kept getting benched whenever Liam wanted to play up front. The final straw came when Derek sat the entire second half, watching Liam blow chance after chance.

They enrolled him in a rival club the next day.

Greg's reaction was volcanic. "Derek's dad can't handle the truth," he spat at practice. "His kid wasn't as good as he thought."

But the scoreboards told the real story. Without Derek, the Predators' losses piled up—and so did the empty spots on their bench.

The Final Straw

By fourteen, Liam was going through the motions.

The Predators were crumbling. Players drifted away—some quietly, others mid-season—tired of the favoritism, the screaming, the suffocating pressure. Parents exchanged glances on the sidelines, their murmurs growing louder with every loss.

Then one night, as they loaded gear into the trunk under the stadium lights, Liam shattered the silence.

"I'm done."

Greg froze. "What?"

"I don't want to play anymore." Liam kept his eyes on the pavement, shoulders hunched.

A harsh laugh. "Don't be ridiculous. You've got real potential—"

"No, I don't!" Liam's voice cracked. "I'm not special. And I don't even like it anymore."

Greg's jaw worked soundlessly. Ten years of drills, tournaments, sacrifices—all leading to this moment in a half-empty parking lot.

And suddenly, the truth hit him like a missed penalty kick: this dream had always been his.

Reflections & Data Integration

Liam's story plays out on fields across America every season. The "coach's kid" syndrome isn't just about unfair playing time—it erodes the fundamental trust that makes team sports worthwhile. When kids smell a rigged system, they check out.

The numbers don't lie. According to the National Alliance for Youth Sports, poor coaching ranks among the top reasons athletes quit. By age 13, over 70% walk away—many citing favoritisms, burnout, and the soul-crushing pressure to perform.

The tragic irony? Most of these coaches aren't villains. They're well-meaning parents who have lost their way, chased wins or lived vicariously through their children while forgetting the real purpose: creating athletes who love the game long after the final whistle blows.

Interview: A Former Youth Coach's Perspective

To get to the heart of this issue, I sat down with Mark Reynolds, a veteran youth coach who's watched countless promising athletes walk away from the game.

"Parents have no idea the damage they cause by turning sports into a pressure cooker," he told me, leaning forward. "I've had kids—talented kids—confess they could barely breathe from their parents' expectations. We're hemorrhaging potential before these players even hit high school."

When I asked about the root cause, his answer was razor-sharp:

"Ego. Plain and simple. Too many coaches are out there building their trophies instead of building athletes. And when adults make it about themselves?" He shook his head. "The kids always pay the price.

Looking Ahead

Liam's story reveals only part of the broken system in youth soccer. Next, we'll expose how pay-to-play politics sideline kids like Maria—a natural midfielder whose talent means nothing without the correct price tag.

What happens when potential meets poverty?

What happens when clubs prioritize profits over players?

For Maria and thousands like her, the game doesn't end with a whistle. It ends with a bill they can't pay.

Chapter 3: A Scholarship for What?

Maria Flores could weave through defenders like they were standing still—before most kids could even double-knot their cleats.

Her father, Javier, would laugh and say she came into this world with soccer balls in her DNA. He'd grown up playing on dusty Mexican streets with a half-deflated ball, his dreams of going pro ending where the pavement did. But watching Maria play, he felt that old hope spark back to life—this time, through her.

By the age of ten, Maria wasn't just the best in her rec league; she was a phenomenon. Lightning quick. Inventive. Relentless. When she joined pickup games with teenage boys, she didn't just keep up—she dominated. Parents would nudge each other on the sidelines, whispering.

"That girl's special," one murmured to Javier after a tournament. "She belongs in a real club."

Javier nodded; his smile tight. He didn't need the reminder. He'd already done the math.

A Price Too High

The price tags were staggering.

Base club fees started at $ 2,000 – before uniforms, before tournaments, travel, and the hidden cost that pushed some families past $ 5,000 a year.

Javier worked construction by day and stocked shelves by night, but no amount of overtime could bridge that gap.

They pinned their hopes on a scholarship. The club director—a polished former college star who'd built the region's top program—studied Maria's file with detached sympathy.

"Our aid fund is limited," he said, sliding a paper across his desk. "We can offer $500."

Javier's hands stayed in his lap. It was a discount on a dream Maria still couldn't afford.

So, she kept playing rec ball, watching as teammates vanished one by one—their parents' minivans carrying them toward futures measured in cleat costs and hotel fees. Maria's talent didn't fade. Her opportunities did.

The College Myth

The summer Maria turned 13, she and Javier sat in the bleachers at a high school showcase tournament, the air thick with tension and ambition. College scouts prowled the sidelines, clipboards in hand, their eyes tracking only the players wearing elite club crests on their jerseys. The unspoken rule screamed louder than any coach: No club badge? No future.

Javier's hands clenched around the railing. Back in Mexico, talent scouts would have fought to fund a player like Maria. Here? The system required them to pay for the privilege of being noticed.

Maria studied the girls on the field—their crisp passes, their confident runs. She knew she could match them move for move. But as the ball ricocheted between players who'd had years of private coaching, one bitter question settled in her chest:

How many of them were truly better—and how many just had parents who could afford to make them look that way?

A Fading Dream

At fifteen, Maria stopped pretending.

The chasm between rec league and competitive club soccer had grown too vast—a divide measured in dollars, not talent. College dreams, scouts' glances, scholarship hopes—these belonged to kids whose parents could buy them visibility.

When she told Javier, his slow nod carried the weight of buried dreams.

"You could have been special," he murmured, the words hanging between them like the ghost of a life unlived.

Maria studied her worn cleats. "Maybe," she said.

Just maybe.

Reflections & Data Integration

Maria's story isn't an exception—it's the rule. Across America, financial barriers prevent countless talented kids from playing sports, while the pay-to-play system continues to expand.

The numbers tell the brutal truth:

• Income = Access: The Aspen Institute reveals family wealth as the #1 predictor of sports participation

• 3x GA: Kids from households with incomes of $100,000+ are nearly three times more likely to play than their lower-income peers.

• 2B Industry: club soccer has become a profit-driven enterprise where money routinely outweighs merit.

Yet for all this spending, American soccer still struggles to produce elite talent – proof that when we prioritize wallets over ability, everyone loses.

Interview: The Broken Pipeline

I sat down with Ryan Dempsey, a former Division I coach who's spent decades watching the system fail players like Maria. His frustration was palpable.

"We're hemorrhaging talent," he said, leaning forward. "While European clubs actively scout and develop promising players, we've built a paywall that keeps kids out unless their parents can write checks."

When I asked about progress, his laugh held no humor.

"Change? It's glacial. The truth is simple—until we stop conflating privilege with potential, we'll keep losing generations of kids who should be dominating the world stage."

Looking Ahead

Maria's story reveals the brutal truth: pay-to-play isn't just excluding talent—it's bankrupting families who invest in the dream.

Next: Jake's Story—the Hidden Cost of Chasing Scholarships.

His parents drained college funds, took second jobs, and sacrificed vacations. But when the promised opportunities never materialized, they were left with one burning question:

Was it ever really about soccer—or were they funding someone else's business model?

Chapter 4: Jake and the Hidden Costs

Jake Mercer checked every box of a rising soccer star—at least on paper.

By ten, he'd earned a spot on one of the state's elite club teams. His parents, Eric and Lisa, heard the same pitch countless families swallow whole:

"Club soccer isn't an expense—it's an investment. The only path to college play."

So, they invested. Deeply.

Vacations vanished. Car payments stretched. College savings bled into tournament fees. The family budget became a spreadsheet of sacrifices, all pinned to one unshakable belief:

Jake's talent was their golden ticket.

The Cost of the Dream

By fourteen, Jake was logging more flight miles than family meals.

$10,000 a year. ECNL showcases. Four-a-day tournament schedules. The Mercer family calendar revolved around soccer seasons, their savings account draining with every "elite" opportunity.

Then came the cracks.

"I'm exhausted, Mom."

Lisa dismissed it at first—just a phase. But when the boy who once sneaked out at dawn to practice volleys started making excuses to skip training, her stomach dropped.

The confession came in a quiet moment: "I don't love it anymore."

Panic surged through her. Not now. Not after all they'd sacrificed.

"Just push through to college," she urged, voice tight. "It'll pay off."

But as Jake turned away, the unspoken question hung between them:

Would it?

The Scholarship Reality

At 16, Jake was recruited by several Division II and III colleges, but there were no full-ride scholarships on the table.

When his parents sat down with one of the coaches, they finally grasped the reality.

"Soccer scholarships aren't like those for football or basketball," the coach explained. "Even at Division I, most players receive only partial scholarships. Full rides are rare."

Eric and Lisa were stunned. They had spent five figures annually for eight years, all with the hope that a scholarship would eventually cover their expenses.

Now, they were looking at a possible $5,000 per year in aid—maybe.

It didn't take a math genius to realize that they had spent far more on club soccer than they would ever recoup in scholarships.

The Breaking Point

The decision came on an ordinary Sunday afternoon, shattering eight years of expectations with one quiet sentence:

"I don't want to play in college."

Lisa's hands froze mid-motion. "But... after everything we—"

"I just want to be normal." Jake's voice was steady, final.

The silence that followed swallowed years of sacrifice—the drained savings, the missed birthdays, the endless highway miles between tournaments. All those hotel rooms, all that hope, now reduced to receipts in a filing cabinet.

And in that moment, Lisa understood the cruel truth they'd refused to see:

This wasn't Jake's abandoned dream. It was theirs.

Reflections & Data Integration

Jake's story is one that unfolds across the country every year.

The NCAA reports that less than 1.3% of boys playing high school soccer will go on to play at the Division I level. Even fewer will receive significant scholarship money. NCAA soccer teams are allocated only 9.9 scholarships per team for men, which must be divided among an average roster of 29 players.

Families often spend far more on club soccer than they ever receive in scholarships.

Interview: The Business of False Promises

When I asked Coach Anthony Reyes about the scholarship myth, the veteran recruiter's laugh held no humor.

"Clubs aren't selling soccer training," he said, leaning forward. "They're selling parental hope. Toss out 'college scholarship' and watch families mortgage their futures."

The numbers? Brutal.

"Maybe 1% break even. The rest?" He spread his hands wide. They pay ten thousand dollars a year for the privilege of heartbreak.

Looking Ahead

Jake's story reveals the hidden truth about youth soccer: the system isn't selling development—it's selling hope at a premium.

But what happens to kids who aren't chasing scholarships? To those who just want to play without mortgaging their childhood?

Next: Tyrone's story—the last rec league holdout.

When pay-to-play swallowed his local league whole, this talented kid faced a brutal choice: pay up or walk away. The tragedy? He wasn't the one who decided to quit. The game quit on him.

Chapter 5: Tyrone and the Vanishing Rec League

Tyrone Johnson counted down the days until soccer season.

At twelve, he wasn't the star player—just a kid who loved the game. The thud of the ball against his cleats. The wind rushing past as he charged toward goal. The way his team would pile together after a win, sweaty and grinning.

For Tyrone, soccer wasn't about scholarships or scouts. It was pure joy.

Then came the notice:

"City Youth Soccer League - DISCONTINUED"

Tyrone's stomach dropped. "But... how?"

Monique scrolled through the empty registration page. "Not enough players signed up."

It made no sense. Six years ago, the fields had been packed—dozens of teams, Saturday morning chaos, the smell of fresh-cut grass. Now? Silence.

When Coach Patel explained, his voice was tired:

Club soccer is bleeding us dry. Kids think they need fancy uniforms and travel teams to play."

Tyrone stared at his worn cleats. When did having fun become a requirement for a credit card?

The Paywall

Monique pulled up the club soccer website that night, clinging to hope.

The numbers hit like a gut punch: $2,500—before uniforms, before hotels, before gas for tournaments. Her nurse's salary barely covered rent and groceries as it was.

The club director's voice was polite but firm when she called:

"Our scholarship fund covers maybe 20% at most."

Monique's fingers tightened around the phone. She'd heard this script before—the same one that had sidelined Maria years earlier. The math was simple:

No money. No soccer.

Tyrone's cleats stayed in the closet that season. Not because he wasn't good enough.

Because his mother's paycheck wasn't big enough.

Nowhere Left to Play

That autumn, Tyrone came home to empty afternoons.

He'd still kick a ball against the garage door sometimes, imagining defenders dodging. But the organized games—the ref's whistle, the team huddles, the orange slices after matches—had vanished along with the league.

Club kids disappeared to weekend tournaments. Neighborhood friends moved on. The park fields, once buzzing with weekend games, grew quiet.

Soccer—the people's game, the street game, the every-kid's game—had become a privilege.

And Tyrone?

He hung up his cleats for good.

Reflections & Data Integration

Tyrone's story isn't an isolated case—it's a symptom of a broken system.

The Disappearing Game

Recreational leagues are vanishing. According to the Aspen Institute, youth sports participation has dropped 15% since 2010—with low-income families hit hardest

Club soccer is booming—for the privileged. So-called "nonprofit" clubs now charge $3,000+ per season, pricing out working-class kids

The American Paradox

While soccer thrives as the people's game in Brazil and Argentina, the U.S. has turned it into a paywalled sport—where talent matters less than a parent's credit score.

Interview: The Cost of Exclusion

I spoke with Coach James Holloway, a former high school coach who witnessed the demise of his local rec league.

"The moment club soccer took over, rec leagues died," he said. "And the kids who suffered the most were those who couldn't afford the club fees."

When I asked him what the solution was, he sighed.

"We need to bring back affordable soccer," he said. "Otherwise, we're losing an entire generation of kids."

Looking Ahead

Tyrone's story is about access—or the lack of it. But what happens when even the best players in the country struggle with the system?

In the next chapter, we meet Dante and the Broken Development Pathway—a talented teenager who did everything right, only to discover that in U.S. soccer, the road to success isn't designed for players like him.

Chapter 6: Dante and the Broken Development Pathway

Dante Carter was the kind of player who could change a game in an instant. At 16, he possessed everything: speed, vision, and technical skill. His coaches referred to him as a natural. His teammates knew that when the game was on the line, the ball needed to be at his feet.

He wasn't just good; he was special.

But in America, talent alone wasn't enough.

The Wrong ZIP Code

Dante grew up in a working-class neighborhood outside of Atlanta. His parents, Malcolm and Denise, were supportive but realistic. They couldn't afford expensive club soccer, but they believed in their son.

Dante first gained attention playing pickup games at the local park. A coach from a mid-tier club team spotted him and offered him a spot on their roster with a partial scholarship.

It wasn't a perfect situation—his family still had to scrape together money for travel and gear—but it was an opportunity.

Over the next few years, Dante competed in state and regional tournaments, proving himself against kids who had been in the club system since they were six. Coaches and parents would shake their heads as they watched him play.

"If this kid were at [big-name club], he'd be on a national team already," they'd say.

But that was the problem. Dante wasn't part of one of the elite Development Academy clubs. And in American soccer, if you're not in the right system, you don't exist.

The College and Pro Blockade

At 17, Dante began thinking about his future. He wanted to play soccer in college, but his club team lacked the connections that top academies had. He also hoped to play professionally, but in the U.S., there was no direct pipeline for working-class kids like him.

In most of the world, clubs scout and invest in raw talent. However, the U.S. pay-to-play model creates artificial barriers. Instead of teams funding players, families were expected to fund the teams. Dante watched as players with less talent but more financial resources got scouted simply because they were part of the right club.

The Overseas Gamble

One night, Dante's dad sat him down. "If you want to make it, you might need to leave," he said. It was a conversation more and more talented American kids were having. They weren't being developed at home, so they were looking abroad.

Dante started reaching out to lower-division European academies. A coach from a small club in Portugal expressed interest. "We'd love to have him train with us," the coach wrote. "However, he'll need to cover his own expenses."

The cost for the first year was $10,000. Dante looked at his dad, and he didn't even need to ask. It wasn't happening.

A Dead End

By the time Dante graduated from high school, he had received a few small colleges offers, but none of them were full-ride scholarships. There were no professional opportunities on the horizon either.

At 18, he decided to stop chasing the dream. Another talented player was lost, not because he wasn't good enough, but because the American system wasn't designed to support players like him.

Reflections & Data Integration

Dante's story is a symptom of a broken soccer development system. The U.S. Soccer Development Academy, now known as MLS Next, was intended to create a professional pipeline, but it primarily serves kids from wealthier families.

In contrast to other countries, where clubs scout and invest in talent, the U.S. system expects players to pay thousands just to be seen. This pay-to-play model creates significant barriers for talented players from lower socioeconomic backgrounds.

The result is that the U.S. consistently fails to produce world-class players, despite having a large pool of potential talent.

Interview: The Flawed Pipeline

I spoke with Coach Miguel Herrera, who has worked with both American and European academies.

"In Spain or Germany, clubs identify the best young players and develop them without cost," he explained. "In the U.S., the best kids often get left behind because they can't afford to be seen."

When I asked him if the U.S. could ever compete at the highest level, he shook his head.

"Not until we stop making talent pay to play," he said.

Looking Ahead

Dante's story is about talent being wasted. But what about the kids who never even get the chance to fail?

In the next chapter, we meet Mia and the Missing Girls—a young girl who loved soccer, until she realized the game wasn't built for her.

Chapter 7: Mia and the Missing Girls

Mia Alvarez had always been faster than the boys. As a little girl, she played in the street with her older brother and his friends, outrunning them, outworking them, never backing down from a challenge.

But when she turned 12, something changed. The boys continued playing, while the girls disappeared.

Nowhere to Go

Mia had played in the city's recreational league since she was five. Every season, she was the best player on her team. However, at 12, the league shut down its girls' division.

"Not enough sign-ups," the director told her mom.

Mia could still play—with the boys. But suddenly, things felt different.

At first, she held her own. By 13, though, the boys had grown bigger, stronger, and more physical. Coaches stopped putting her in important positions. Some of the boys ignored her, while others made her feel like she didn't belong.

"Shouldn't you be playing volleyball?" one of them laughed after a rough tackle.

The worst part was that the girls who had played alongside her were just... gone. Some had tried club soccer, but most had quit altogether. And once you quit, it was almost impossible to come back.

The Pay Gap in Youth Sports

Mia's mom, Carmen, looked into club soccer. She had heard the same thing from other parents: "If you want Mia to play in high school, she needs to be in club." However, when she saw the cost, she felt sick. The annual fee was $3,000, not including uniforms, tournament fees, or travel expenses.

Carmen made just enough to provide for her family, so soccer wasn't an option. She later learned that the dropout rate for girls in sports is nearly twice that of boys. The biggest reason? Cost.

The Silent Exit

At 14, Mia stopped playing soccer. Her mom didn't realize it at first. There was no dramatic decision, no big moment—just a slow fading away. Mia still loved the game; she watched matches on TV and juggled a ball in the backyard. However, there was nowhere left for her to play.

By high school, Mia's identity as an athlete had been erased. Her brother, meanwhile, continued to play. His team received new uniforms, traveled to out-of-state tournaments, and even had college scouts attending their games.

The only difference between them? He had access to the right opportunities. She didn't.

Reflections & Data Integration

Mia's story isn't unique. Girls are leaving youth sports at alarming rates. According to the Women's Sports Foundation, by age 14, girls drop out of sports at twice the rate of boys.

Cost is one of the biggest barriers. While families are now spending more on girls' sports than boys' sports in some areas, such as travel and lessons, the overall participation rate remains lower for girls. This disparity often stems from societal expectations and financial constraints, as families may be less likely to invest heavily in sports for daughters compared to sons.

The gender gap in youth sports leads to fewer female athletes, fewer female coaches, and fewer role models for young girls. This lack of representation can discourage girls from participating in sports, contributing to higher dropout rates.

Interview: Where Are the Girls?

I spoke with Coach Brianna Lewis, a former college player now working in youth development.

"The system isn't built for girls," she said bluntly. "Clubs prioritize boys' teams and invest in their development first. Girls' teams are often an afterthought."

I asked her what the solution was.

"We need better funding for girls' programs," she said. "We need recreational leagues that don't disappear. And we need to stop treating girls' sports as optional."

Looking Ahead

Mia's story is about exclusion—not just based on money, but on gender. But what happens when a coach, someone who should be there for the kids, makes it all about himself?

In the next chapter, we meet Coach Brad and the Self-Serving Coach—a man who viewed youth soccer not as a way to develop kids, but as a means to build his own status.

Chapter 8: Coach Brad and the Self-Serving Coach

Brad Weston strutted onto the field like he owned it. He wasn't just a youth soccer coach—he was the coach, or so he liked to tell people.

With his perfectly pressed club jacket, mirrored sunglasses, and clipboard full of drills he had found online, Coach Brad saw himself as a tactical genius. He spoke about formations as if he were coaching in the Champions League and name-dropped college scouts he had never actually met.

Despite his self-importance, there was one thing Brad didn't really care about: the kids.

The Wrong Priorities

Brad coached a U-13 club team as part of a well-known local program, but he wasn't coaching for the right reasons. He wasn't there to develop players or teach life lessons. Instead, Brad was coaching to enhance his own reputation.

He prioritized picking the biggest, fastest kids, even if they weren't the most skilled. He ignored players who weren't obvious superstars. Brad focused on winning over development, often running up the score on weaker teams.

While Brad wasn't a bad coach in the traditional sense—his teams won games—he wasn't building players. He was building a resume.

Destroying Kids' Confidence

Brad coached a U-13 club team as part of a well-known local program, but he wasn't coaching for the right reasons. He wasn't there to develop players or teach life lessons. Instead, Brad was coaching to enhance his own reputation.

He prioritized picking the biggest, fastest kids, even if they weren't the most skilled. He ignored players who weren't obvious superstars. Brad focused on winning over development, often running up the score on weaker teams.

While Brad wasn't a bad coach in the traditional sense—his teams won games—he wasn't building players. He was building a resume.

The Parent Puppeteer

Brad wasn't just bad for kids—he was bad for parents, too. He played favorites, not based on talent, but on which families could help him.

If a dad owned a business that could sponsor the team, his kid would get more playing time. If a mom worked at the local college, her son was suddenly touted as a "future prospect." If a parent questioned him, their kid would mysteriously find themselves stuck on the bench.

Brad knew how to manipulate. He told parents what they wanted to hear, making them believe he held the keys to their child's future. Many parents trusted him because they didn't understand the youth soccer system. They didn't realize that Brad had no real connections—his "scouting contacts" were just casual conversations at coaching clinics. The same kids he praised to their faces were often ignored at practice.

The Exit Strategy

Brad's self-serving coaching had consequences. Liam quit soccer, and several talented players left for different clubs. As time passed, parents began to realize that Brad wasn't the expert he pretended to be.

Eventually, the club director replaced him. However, it was too late for many of the kids. Some never returned to the sport. Meanwhile, Brad simply moved to another club, repeating the cycle.

Reflections & Data Integration

Brad's story isn't rare. Youth sports are filled with coaches who put themselves first.

According to the National Alliance for Youth Sports, about 70% of kids quit organized sports by age 13. One of the biggest reasons is bad coaching experiences. The "winning-over-development" mentality often pushes out late bloomers and technical players in favor of short-term success.

The pay-to-play system enables self-serving coaches because clubs aren't always looking for the best coaches; they're looking for coaches who can bring in paying families.

Interview: The Damage Bad Coaches Do

I spoke with Coach Mark Reynolds, who has spent 20 years coaching at both the club and high school levels.

"Bad coaching doesn't just hurt kids in the moment—it pushes them out of the game forever," he told me. "I've seen great kids quit because they had a coach who only cared about winning or who played favorites with parents. That's the real tragedy."

Looking Ahead

Brad's story is about youth coaches who treat kids like a stepping stone. But what happens when the entire system treats soccer like a business instead of a sport?

In the next chapter, we meet Chris and the Business of Soccer—a father who thought he was signing his son up for a game but instead found himself trapped in a financial machine.

Chapter 9: Chris and the Business of Soccer

Chris Morgan just wanted his son to play soccer. When his six-year-old, Ethan, showed an early love for the game, Chris did what any supportive parent would do—he signed him up for the local recreation league. It was simple: $80 for the season, Saturday morning games, a team T-shirt, and a volunteer coach.

Ethan loved it, and for a while, it was enough. However, one of the other parents pulled Chris aside and said, "You should really think about getting Ethan into club soccer." Chris had never heard of club soccer. He assumed that if his son was good enough, he'd make his high school team one day, maybe even earn a college scholarship.

But what he was about to learn was that soccer wasn't just a game anymore—it was a business.

The Sales Pitch

A few weeks later, Chris took Ethan to a club tryout. The experience was overwhelming. There were hundreds of kids on the fields, all wearing different gear from various clubs. Coaches walked around with clipboards, acting like talent scouts. Parents whispered on the sidelines, discussing which club had the best "pathway" to college. Chris had no idea what any of it meant.

Ethan made the team, but instead of congratulations, Chris received an invoice. The cost for the season was $2,500, not including uniforms, tournament fees, or travel expenses. Chris hesitated, but the club's director assured him, "This is an investment in Ethan's future." So Chris paid.

What he didn't realize was that he wasn't paying for Ethan to play; he was paying to keep Ethan in the system.

The Never-Ending Fees

The first year, Chris accepted the costs as part of having a "serious" athlete. However, as time passed, the expenses started piling up. There was a new uniform package every two years, costing $500. Mandatory summer camps added another $300. Tournaments out of state were $1,000 per trip. And then there was the winter indoor league, which wasn't included in the initial fees, costing an additional $400.

Chris wasn't wealthy. He made a decent living, but soccer started to feel like a second mortgage. Then came the next level of pressure. One day, another parent warned him, "If Ethan wants to play in high school, he needs to be in the 'Elite' program." Chris checked the price: $5,000 per year. At that point, he had a choice—pay more or risk Ethan falling behind.

The Business Model of Pay-to-Play

Chris had unknowingly entered the youth soccer machine. The more parents were willing to pay, the higher the costs seemed to get. Clubs justified these fees by claiming they offered a "path to college," even though less than 5% of high school players actually received college scholarships. Development wasn't always the goal; keeping paying families happy was.

Chris wasn't alone. Families across the country were drowning in soccer expenses. Meanwhile, in countries like Spain, Germany, and Brazil, kids like Ethan played for free in professional academies. There, clubs scouted and developed talent because producing top players was their investment. In contrast, in the U.S., parents were the investors.

The Breaking Point

By the time Ethan was 14, Chris had spent nearly $20,000 on soccer. And for what? He started noticing things. The kids getting the most playing time weren't always the best—but their parents were often club sponsors. The club directors seemed more interested in whether Chris could afford another year than in Ethan's progress. Despite all the money spent, there was no real pathway to professional soccer.

Chris had enough. He pulled Ethan out of club soccer. Ethan was initially crushed, but Chris found him a local independent training program—a fraction of the cost, with no false promises. By high school, Ethan was still playing and loving the game. Chris felt relief; he had finally escaped the business of soccer.

Reflections & Data Integration

Chris's story is one that plays out in households across the U.S. The average cost of youth club soccer ranges from $2,500 to $5,000 per year, with elite levels often exceeding these figures. However, less than 1% of youth soccer players will go pro. The system sells a dream that only a tiny fraction will ever achieve.

Families often feel trapped, spending thousands just to "stay in the system." This financial burden can be overwhelming, as families like Chris's are convinced that these investments are necessary for their child's future success in soccer.

Interview: The Pay-to-Play Trap

I spoke with David Ross, a former club director who left the system after 15 years.

"The whole model is built on money," he admitted. "Most clubs aren't actually developing talent. They're just collecting fees."

When I asked if things would ever change, he sighed. "Not as long as parents keep paying."

Looking Ahead

Chris's story is about parents being sold a dream that rarely comes true. But what about the clubs themselves? In the next chapter, we explore how soccer clubs are operating as businesses first, with soccer programs often taking a secondary role.

Chapter 10: The Club Soccer Industry

Chris had pulled Ethan out of club soccer, but the machine kept running. It had to. Because club soccer in America wasn't just about developing players—it was a multi-billion dollar industry. For every family like Chris's who opted out, ten more were lining up, wallets open, hoping their kid was the next star.

How Soccer Became a Business

In the 1980s and 90s, youth soccer in the U.S. was mostly recreational. Kids played for fun, and the best of them found their way onto high school and college teams. However, with the rise of club soccer, everything changed. Parents sought higher levels of competition, and clubs realized they could charge thousands of dollars per year. As a result, youth soccer became less about access and more about exclusivity.

By the early 2000s, club soccer had overtaken recreational leagues, and the cost of participation skyrocketed. Today, the system is clear: if you don't pay, you don't play. If you can't afford club soccer, your chances of progressing drop significantly. If you leave the system, it's nearly impossible to re-enter. All of this exists while the U.S. still struggles internationally in soccer. The spending continues to increase, but the results remain unchanged.

The Business Model of Club Soccer

Club soccer operates on a simple economic principle: scarcity creates demand. By making families believe that club soccer is the only pathway to success, clubs have monetized opportunity itself. This business model relies on several key pillars:

Expansion of Non-Profit Clubs That Operate Like Businesses

There has been a dramatic rise in "non-profit" club teams that bring in millions of dollars in fees annually. Many of these clubs are legally non-profits but operate as for-profit businesses, paying high salaries to directors and coaches while charging families excessive fees. Over the past 20 years, the number of these clubs has tripled, while true recreational leagues have declined.

The Myth of the "Pathway"

Clubs promote the idea that their players will have a higher chance of playing college or professional soccer. However, in reality, only about 5% of high school soccer players go on to play in college, and less than 1% of club soccer players ever make it to professional leagues. Despite this, clubs continue to sell the idea that expensive academies are the only way forward.

Pay-to-Win Tournament Culture

Clubs enter high-cost, high-profile tournaments to give families the illusion of exposure. Many of these tournaments are pay-to-enter showcases, where teams compete against each other for nothing more than bragging rights. Some families spend over $10,000 per year traveling to tournaments with no real long-term benefit.

Keeping Families on the Hook

Clubs often introduce "Elite" programs that cost even more, giving families the impression that higher fees equal better opportunities. Some clubs create artificial promotion/relegation systems, where players must keep paying just to maintain their spot. Instead of investing in player development, clubs invest in marketing to recruit more paying families.

The High Cost of Entry

Due to this business model, soccer has become one of the most expensive youth sports in the United States. The average cost of club soccer ranges from $2,500 to $5,000 per year, with some elite academies charging over $10,000 annually. This high cost prices out lower-income families, limiting diversity in the sport.

In contrast, soccer is nearly free in countries like Brazil, Argentina, and Germany, where professional clubs invest in youth development. The result is that the U.S. spends more money than ever on youth soccer yet still struggles to develop world-class players.

Interview: Where Is the Money Going?

I spoke with Tom Lawson, a former club director who worked inside the system for over a decade.

"Clubs aren't focused on developing the best players," he admitted. "They're focused on attracting the most paying families."

I asked him where the money goes. "Some of it goes to coaches, but a lot of it goes to facilities, tournaments, and overhead," he explained. "Most clubs aren't reinvesting in players—they're reinvesting in their brand."

When I asked him if the system would ever change, he laughed. "Not unless parents stop paying. And that's not happening anytime soon."

Looking Ahead

The club soccer industry is designed to serve itself first, not the players. But what happens when an entire group of kids—lower-income and inner-city youth—never even get a chance to play? In the next chapter, we explore the barriers that keep America's most talented kids out of soccer.

Chapter 11: The Missing Generation

In a neighborhood park on the south side of Chicago, a group of kids played soccer with a half-inflated ball. They wore mismatched jerseys—some from European clubs, some from local high schools, and some just plain T-shirts. There were no club banners, no parents on the sidelines dissecting strategy, and no uniforms that cost hundreds of dollars.

Yet, the talent was undeniable. Seventeen-year-old Javier Gutierrez weaved through defenders with ease, his movements smooth and instinctual. He had never trained in a formal academy or played in a high-cost tournament. But anyone watching knew—this kid had something special.

The problem? No one was watching. Javier wasn't in the club system. His family couldn't afford it. And because of that, his path to high-level soccer in the U.S. was almost nonexistent.

This is the story of an entire missing generation of players—kids who could be the future of American soccer but never even get the chance.

The Price of Exclusion

In almost every major soccer country, the best players often come from low-income backgrounds. For example, Pelé grew up in poverty in Brazil, kicking a sock stuffed with rags as his first ball. Diego Maradona was raised in the slums of Buenos Aires, playing street football before being recruited into an academy. Kylian Mbappé came from a working-class neighborhood in France, where local clubs actively scouted and developed talent.

However, in the U.S., where the pay-to-play model dominates, kids like Javier are left behind. Club soccer costs between $2,500 and $5,000 per year, a sum many families cannot afford. High-level teams often require extensive travel, adding thousands in costs. Many clubs don't actively scout lower-income areas; instead, they wait for kids to come to them—with a check in hand. As a result, some of the most naturally gifted players never even step onto a proper field. It's not about talent; it's about access.

AAU Basketball vs. Club Soccer: A Stark Contrast

While soccer locks kids out, another sport has mastered identifying and developing inner-city talent: basketball. AAU basketball is heavily subsidized for top players, with shoe companies, colleges, and sponsors investing in young talent. The best kids don't pay thousands to play—they are recruited. Coaches actively scout underserved areas because they know that's where elite talent often comes from.

This system has helped the U.S. dominate basketball globally. In contrast, soccer remains a suburban, upper-middle-class sport, despite being the world's game. The U.S. isn't short on talent; it's just looking in the wrong places.

The International Model: How Other Countries Get It Right

Unlike the U.S., where families fund youth soccer, the rest of the world takes a different approach. In Europe and South America, professional clubs—not parents—invest in young players. Academies are free, and if a kid has talent, they play. There are no financial barriers. Clubs actively scout talent in lower-income neighborhoods and develop players from a young age. Players don't have to spend years paying into a system; if they're good enough, they rise through the ranks.

This system isn't perfect, but it works. It ensures that talent—not money—determines opportunity.

Interview: A College Coach Speaks Out

I spoke with Coach Adam Benson, a Division I college soccer coach, about the problem.

"We're missing out on incredible players every year," he said. "The best kids in the country aren't necessarily in the club system. But we don't see them because they never get the chance."

When I asked him why clubs don't scout inner-city areas more, his answer was blunt. "Because they don't have to. Parents in wealthier areas are willing to pay. There's no financial incentive to find kids who can't afford it."

I pressed him on whether that would ever change. "Not unless the entire system is rebuilt," he said. "And that's not happening anytime soon."

Javier's Story: What Could Have Been

Javier kept playing pickup soccer and dominated in high school. However, he never got recruited to a big club and never played in the high-profile tournaments where scouts watched. By 18, he was working full-time at his uncle's auto shop. By 20, he had stopped playing altogether.

He could have been the next Clint Dempsey or Christian Pulisic. But Javier's story isn't unique. It happens every single year. Hundreds—maybe thousands—of talented kids never even get a chance.

Looking Ahead

The U.S. will never reach its full potential in soccer until it fixes its broken system. Lower-income kids must have a pathway into high-level soccer. Scouting must expand beyond wealthy suburbs. The pay-to-play model must be replaced with club-funded development programs.

Until then, the U.S. will continue to outspend the world while falling behind on the field. In the next chapter, we'll explore solutions: what can change, what parents can do, and most importantly, is there hope for a better future in American soccer?

Chapter 12: A Broken System—Can It Be Fixed?

Javier Gutierrez should have been playing in a professional academy, competing against the best young players in the country. Instead, he was working 10-hour shifts at his uncle's auto shop, another lost talent in a system that never gave him a chance.

The problem isn't that the U.S. lacks talent; it's that the system isn't designed to find and develop it. So, the question remains: Can American soccer fix what's broken?

The Three Core Problems

If we want to fix U.S. soccer, we first have to acknowledge what's wrong.

The High Cost of Participation

Club soccer costs $2,500 to $5,000 per year on average, creating a significant financial barrier for many families. High-level tournaments and travel add thousands more in hidden costs. There are few scholarships or subsidies, making club soccer primarily a sport for the upper middle class.

Lack of Scouting & Development in Lower-Income Areas

Unlike basketball and football, youth soccer does not prioritize inner-city or lower-income scouting. Clubs rely on families coming to them with money rather than actively searching for talent. In other countries, professional clubs fund development academies for kids regardless of financial status. In the U.S., that responsibility falls on parents.

The Pay-to-Play Incentive Structure

U.S. soccer clubs make money from fees, not player development. There's little financial incentive for clubs to lower costs or scout non-paying players. Many non-profit clubs operate as businesses, using their status to avoid taxes while still charging families excessive fees.

What Other Countries Do Differently

In Europe and South America, soccer is treated as an investment, not a business. Professional clubs actively scout and develop young talent. If a player is good enough, they receive a free education and training at a top academy. National federations support youth development programs. For example, in Germany, the DFB Talentförderprogramm ensures that every region has access to high-level training.

These academies are merit-based, not wealth-based. If you have the skill, you play—no matter your family's income. This model fosters stronger national teams by allowing the best players to rise to the top.

In contrast, the U.S. model invests in families who can afford to pay, not necessarily the most talented players.

Possible Solutions: What Needs to Change?

To create real change, American soccer must shift its priorities.

Expand Free & Low-Cost Development Programs

U.S. Soccer should invest in subsidized academies in underserved areas, similar to those in Europe. Major League Soccer (MLS) clubs need to expand their free academy systems and actively recruit lower-income players. More states should fund state-sponsored soccer initiatives to help kids play without financial barriers.

Hold Non-Profit Clubs Accountable

Many clubs hide behind non-profit status while charging high fees. There should be stricter oversight on where this money goes. More clubs should be required to offer scholarships or reinvest in player development. Parents should demand financial transparency from clubs that claim to be non-profit.

Expand Scouting into Inner Cities & Rural Areas

U.S. Soccer should create national scouting initiatives to identify talent in lower-income areas. More clubs should partner with community-based soccer programs to find players outside of the pay-to-play system. College programs should broaden their recruiting networks to include non-club players.

Interview: A Former Club Director Speaks Out

I spoke with Sarah Whitmore, a former club director who spent 15 years in the industry. She left the system because she was frustrated with how clubs prioritized profits over players.

"I had kids come to me crying because they couldn't afford the fees," she told me. "And there was nothing I could do. My hands were tied."

When I asked her what would fix the system, her answer was clear: "Clubs need to stop operating like businesses and start acting like true development programs. We're losing too many kids just because their families can't pay."

I asked if she thought that would ever happen. "Not unless parents start demanding change," she admitted. "As long as people are willing to pay, clubs will keep charging."

The Role of Parents & Coaches

The club soccer industry won't change on its own. However, parents, coaches, and communities can force the issue.

Parents' Role: Parents need to challenge the pay-to-play model by demanding transparency from clubs. This includes asking for detailed financial reports and ensuring that funds are used for player development rather than just profit.

Coaches' Advocacy: Volunteer coaches must advocate for more accessible programs and push back against club systems that exclude lower-income kids. They can help create community-based initiatives that provide affordable opportunities for all children.

Community Investment: Communities should invest in local recreational leagues to ensure that soccer remains affordable for all kids—not just those who can pay. This can involve collaborating with local organizations to build facilities and provide resources for underprivileged areas.

Change won't happen overnight. But if enough people push back, the system will have to adjust.

Looking Forward

Javier Gutierrez never got his shot. But the next generation still has a chance—if the system is rebuilt to work for all players, not just the ones who can afford it. As this book nears its conclusion, the final chapter will serve as a call to action:

What Can Parents Do Today? Parents can demand transparency from clubs, advocate for more affordable programs, and support community-based initiatives that provide opportunities for underprivileged children.

How Can Coaches, Directors, and Community Leaders Make a Difference? Coaches and directors can push for more inclusive programs, while community leaders can invest in local recreational leagues and advocate for policy changes that support accessible soccer.

And Most Importantly, Will American Soccer Finally Look Itself in the Mirror and Ask: Are We in This for the Right Reasons? The U.S. soccer system must reflect on its priorities and ensure that it values player development and inclusivity over financial gain.

Chapter 13: The Call to Action

Javier Gutierrez didn't quit soccer because he lacked talent. He quit because the system quit on him. It's a story that has played out for decades across the U.S.—a cycle of lost potential, of kids who love the game but are shut out by the very structure meant to support them.

So, the final question remains: What can we do about it? This chapter is not just a conclusion; it's a challenge—a challenge to parents, coaches, club directors, and decision-makers in American soccer.

Parents: The Power to Demand Change

Parents are the consumers in the youth soccer industry. And like any consumer, they have power. If families stop unquestioningly accepting high fees and pay-to-play models, clubs will have no choice but to change.

What Parents Can Do Right Now:

Demand Financial Transparency: Ask clubs where your money goes. Are scholarships available? Is the club truly non-profit, or just using that label?

Support Local Recreational Leagues: If parents commit to keeping rec soccer strong, more kids will have access to the game.

Challenge the Obsession with Club Soccer: Many parents believe that club soccer is the only viable path. It isn't. Encourage your child's passion without assuming that paying thousands is the only way.

Advocate for Change: Push for lower fees, more scholarships, and inclusive policies at the clubs you support.

Parents fund the system. If they push back, the system will be forced to adjust.

Coaches: A Responsibility Beyond the Sidelines

If parents fund the system, coaches shape it. Great coaches put the game and the players first—not their own egos or financial interests. However, too many coaches are caught in the trap of chasing trophies and money, rather than developing players.

What Coaches Must Do:

Coach for the Right Reasons: If you're in it for money, prestige, or power, step aside. Youth sports need coaches who care about kids, not just results.

Prioritize Development Over Winning: The best youth coaches don't focus on short-term victories. They build players for the long haul.

Find Ways to Include All Kids: Offer free clinics. Connect lower-income players to scholarship opportunities. Be the person who opens doors, not the one who closes them.

Challenge Bad Practices Within Clubs: If a club prioritizes money over player development, speak up. The best clubs listen to their coaches.

Youth soccer doesn't need more coaches trying to build their résumés. It requires leaders who care about kids.

Club Directors: Are You in This for the Right Reasons?

To club directors and administrators:

Are you truly serving the mission of soccer development? Or are you just running a business? Many clubs operate under the guise of non-profits while charging thousands of dollars in fees. Too many directors focus on expanding their brand rather than ensuring all kids have access to the game.

What Clubs Need to Do:

Offer More Scholarships and Low-Cost Options: If your club claims to be about "growing the game," prove it. Provide financial aid to families who cannot afford the fees, ensuring that talented players from all backgrounds have access to opportunities for development.

Expand Outreach to Underserved Areas: If your club isn't scouting or recruiting from lower-income communities, it's failing in its mission. Actively seek out talent in these areas and invest in programs that bring soccer to underprivileged children.

Stop Prioritizing Money Over Talent: If a player has potential, find a way to keep them in the game—even if their family can't pay. This means creating pathways for talented players to participate regardless of financial status.

Emphasize Coaching Education: Many clubs prioritize winning over player development. Address this issue by hiring and training coaches who understand the importance of long-term growth. Focus on building players for the future, not just winning short-term games.

If you're running a club, ask yourself: Are we helping players, or just profiting off of them? If the answer is unclear, it's time to reassess your mission.

The Role of U.S. Soccer & MLS: A Call for Structural Change

This issue extends beyond local clubs; it's a systemic failure that originates from the top down. U.S. Soccer and Major League Soccer (MLS) have the resources and influence to reshape the development landscape.

What Needs to Change at the National Level:

Fund Free or Low-Cost Development Academies: Europe and South America have successfully implemented this model. The U.S. must follow suit to ensure that talented players from all backgrounds have access to top-level training.

Expand Scouting into Lower-Income Areas: The best players aren't always in club soccer. Find them where they play—on playgrounds, in schools, and community leagues.

Push MLS Clubs to Invest in Their Youth Programs: More MLS clubs should have free academies that don't require families to pay. This aligns with international models, where professional clubs invest heavily in youth development.

Hold Clubs Accountable for Excessive Fees: If a club claims to be non-profit but charges thousands, U.S. Soccer should investigate where the money is going. This ensures that clubs prioritize player development over profit.

The U.S. will never be a global soccer powerhouse if it continues to prioritize wealth over talent. Actual development requires real investment.

A Final Message to Every Soccer Advocate

This book began with stories—stories of kids left behind, of broken promises, of a system that rewards those who can pay while neglecting those who can't. But this isn't just a book of problems; it's a book of solutions.

It's a call to

Parents: Demand better for your kids. Challenge the status quo and advocate for more affordable and inclusive programs.

Coaches: Put players before trophies. Focus on long-term development rather than short-term wins.

Club Directors: Prioritize access over profit. Invest in programs that ensure all children can participate, regardless of financial background.

U.S. Soccer: Take Concrete Steps Toward Inclusion. Implement policies that promote diversity and accessibility, ensuring every child has the opportunity to participate in play.

Ultimately, soccer should belong to everyone. The next Javier Gutierrez is out there. Will we let him slip through the cracks? Or will we finally build a system where every kid has a chance to play? The future of U.S. soccer depends on the answer. It's time to decide.

Epilogue: Looking to the Future

The lights flickered above a small, worn-down soccer field in a neighborhood most club scouts had never set foot in. A group of kids played under the dim glow, their laughter echoing off the chain-link fence. Their jerseys didn't match. Their cleats were hand-me-downs. But their talent? It was undeniable.

Somewhere among them was a future star. But would anyone notice

This book has explored the flaws in the American soccer system—how pay-to-play has excluded too many kids, how talent identification has failed, and how financial considerations have taken priority over player development.

So, where do we go from here?

The answer isn't simple. But it starts with a shift in perspective, priorities, and action.

The Crossroads of American Soccer

Right now, U.S. soccer stands at a crossroads.

One Path Leads to More of the Same: A system where only wealthy kids can afford to play at a high level, where talented players are overlooked because they can't pay thousands in club fees, and where the U.S. continues to fall short on the international stage.

The Other Path Leads to Real Change: A future where soccer is accessible, where clubs prioritize player development over profit, and where the best players, regardless of their financial background, are given the chance to succeed.

Which path we take depends on the choices we make now.

Let's return to a European example.

Two Paths, Two Outcomes: Why Germany Develops World-Class Players—and the U.S. Doesn't

At a dusty park in a small German town, a scout watches a group of kids playing pickup soccer. One boy, perhaps 11 or 12, controls the ball with effortless precision, weaving through defenders as if he were born to play the game. The scout takes note. Within a few months, that same kid is training at a DFB Stützpunkt—one of Germany's 360 regional development centers, where he receives free, professional coaching under the Talentförderprogramm. If he continues to develop, he'll move on to a Bundesliga academy, fully funded, with a direct path to the professional game.

Now, picture a kid with the same raw talent in the United States. Maybe he plays in a neighborhood park in an inner-city community, maybe on a dirt lot in a rural town. No scouts are watching. There are no federation-funded training centers. If his family can't afford the $3,000+ annual price tag for club soccer, his journey is over before it even begins.

This is the fundamental difference between Germany's Talentförderprogramm and the pay-to-play system in the United States. One is built on finding and developing talent, regardless of background. The other is built on financial barriers, limiting the game to those who can afford to buy their way in.

Development Should Be About Talent—Not Money

Germany's model for open access and professional training, and comparing it with the U.S. model:

Germany's Model: Open Access, Professional Training

Between the ages of 11 and 14, Germany identifies its most promising young players and brings them into free, structured training programs. Every DFB training center (Stützpunkt) follows the same curriculum, led by licensed, professional coaches who are trained to develop young players, not just win games. If a player excels, they progress to Bundesliga academies, where training, education, and living expenses are covered.

This approach ensures that talented players from all backgrounds have access to top-level training, regardless of their financial situation. The German system emphasizes technical skills from a young age, focusing on ball control, passing, and manipulation. Additionally, the DFB has implemented a player-centered approach, emphasizing fun and minimal adult interference in younger age groups, which helps keep more children engaged in the sport.

Key Features of German Youth Development:

Free Training Programs: Talented players are identified and brought into free training programs at a young age.

Standardized Curriculum: All DFB training centers adhere to a uniform curriculum, ensuring consistent development nationwide.

Professional Coaches: Coaches are trained to focus on player development rather than just winning games.

Bundesliga Academies: Successful players progress to fully funded Bundesliga academies, providing a clear pathway to professional soccer.

The U.S. Model: Pay-to-Play, Unequal Opportunity

In contrast, the U.S. model is characterized by a pay-to-play system that often excludes talented players from lower-income backgrounds. Key issues include:

No National Scouting Network: There is no comprehensive scouting network for lower-income kids. If they aren't in an expensive soccer club, they often go unnoticed.

Inconsistent Coaching Quality: The quality of coaching is inconsistent, with many youth teams led by unlicensed coaches who prioritize winning over player development.

Parental Financial Burden: Instead of clubs investing in young players, parents have to fund their child's soccer dreams. If they can't, the dream ends.

Scouting: Finding the Best vs. Finding Those Who Can Pay

Germany's system searches for talent everywhere—from small-town clubs to inner-city playgrounds. Scouts are paid to find the best players and bring them into the development pipeline. In the U.S., youth players have to pay to be seen. Clubs charge thousands of dollars to play in "elite" leagues and showcases where college or professional scouts might be watching. If you don't have the money, you're invisible.

Coaching: Developing Players vs. Keeping Customers

In Germany, coaches at every level follow a unified national curriculum designed to develop technical and tactical skills. They aren't focused on immediate results or winning youth tournaments—they are building professional players for the future. In the United States, the quality of coaching varies significantly. Many youth coaches lack formal training or licensure. Worse, many are financially dependent on keeping players in their program, creating an incentive to hold onto kids rather than push them to the next level.

The Results: Who Wins in the Long Run?

Germany's free, merit-based system has produced generations of world-class players. The 2014 World Cup-winning team included stars like Thomas Müller and Manuel Neuer—players who came through the Talentförderprogramm at no cost to their families. Meanwhile, the U.S. continues to struggle on the men's side. Despite spending more money per capita on youth soccer than almost any country, the U.S. men's national team has never reached a World Cup final. American players struggle to break into top European leagues at the same rate as their South American and European counterparts.

Why? Because Too Many Talented Kids Never Even Got the Chance to Develop

They were priced out. If the U.S. adopted Germany's system, the country would be developing world-class players at the same rate as France, Brazil, or Argentina. The talent exists—but the system isn't built to find it. Until the

U.S. removes financial barriers, professionalizes youth coaching, and creates an accurate scouting and development pipeline, it will continue to fall behind. Soccer is called "the beautiful game" because it belongs to everyone. It's time for American soccer to reflect on its priorities: Is the goal to develop players or to generate revenue?

A Future Worth Fighting For

Imagine a world where every kid, regardless of income, can play at a competitive level. A world where talent, not money, determines opportunity. A world where the U.S. finally produces world-class players from all backgrounds.

This future is possible. But it won't happen on its own. It will take collective effort and commitment from various stakeholders:

Parents Demanding Better: Parents must challenge the status quo and advocate for more affordable and inclusive programs. They should demand transparency from clubs and push for policies that prioritize player development over profit.

Coaches Prioritizing Kids Over Trophies: Coaches need to focus on long-term player development rather than short-term wins. This means emphasizing technical skills and character development over immediate results.

Club Directors Making the Game More Accessible: Club directors should work to reduce financial barriers by offering scholarships, low-cost options, and expanding outreach to underserved areas.

U.S. Soccer Investing in Real, Meaningful Development: U.S. Soccer must invest in programs that identify and develop talent from all backgrounds, similar to international models like Germany's Talentförderprogramm.

Change is never easy. But for the future of American soccer, it's necessary.

The Final Challenge

Somewhere right now, a kid is kicking a ball against the side of an apartment building. No fancy cleats. No expensive training. Just pure love for the game. That kid could be the future of American soccer. But only if we give them the chance.

So, the final challenge isn't just for clubs, parents, or U.S. Soccer. It's for you. What can you do to improve soccer? Ultimately, the fate of the game isn't decided by the system. It's decided by the people willing to fight for it.

The Journey Continues...

This book may be finished, but the work isn't. If you care about making soccer more accessible, start now:

Get Involved in Your Local Community: Volunteer, coach, advocate for lower costs. Every small action can make a difference in providing opportunities for underprivileged children.

Challenge Your Club or League to Become More Inclusive: Request Scholarships and Demand Transparency. Ensure that clubs prioritize player development over profit.

Support Organizations That Help Lower-Income Kids Play: Donate to or volunteer with organizations that provide soccer opportunities to children who cannot afford them.

Speak Up: Change begins when people refuse to accept the status quo. Use your voice to advocate for a more inclusive and accessible soccer environment.

The system won't fix itself. But together, we can build a better future for the game. One where every kid—regardless of their financial situation, background, or social status—has a chance to play. The ball is at our feet. Now, it's time to take the shot.

www.ingramcontent.com/pod-product-compliance
Lightning Source LLC
Chambersburg PA
CBHW060123050426
42448CB00010B/2009